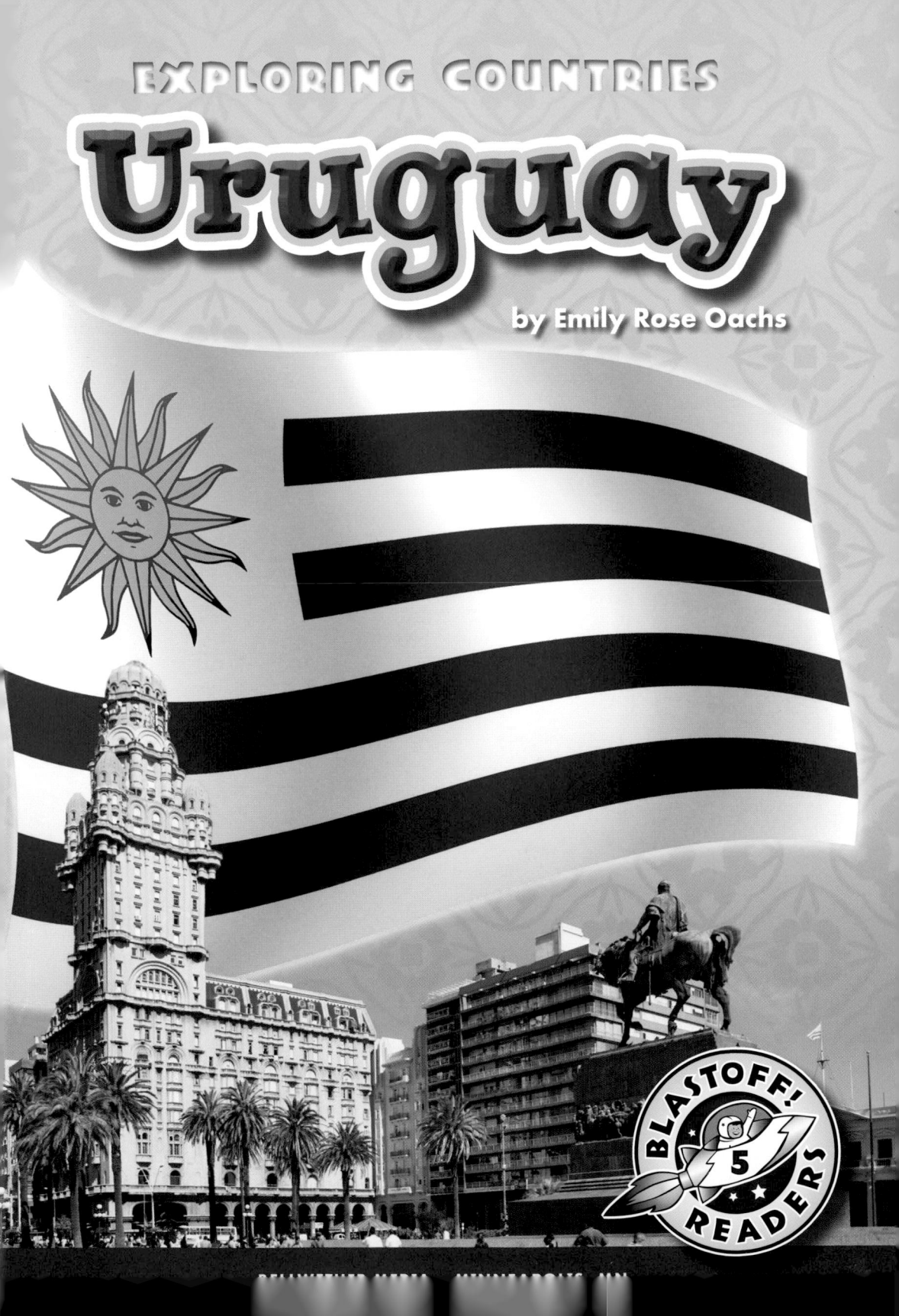

EXPLORING COUNTRIES

Uruguay

by Emily Rose Oachs

BLASTOFF! READERS 5

Note to Librarians, Teachers, and Parents:

Blastoff! Readers are carefully developed by literacy experts and combine standards-based content with developmentally appropriate text.

Level 1 provides the most support through repetition of high-frequency words, light text, predictable sentence patterns, and strong visual support.

Level 2 offers early readers a bit more challenge through varied simple sentences, increased text load, and less repetition of high-frequency words.

Level 3 advances early-fluent readers toward fluency through increased text and concept load, less reliance on visuals, longer sentences, and more literary language.

Level 4 builds reading stamina by providing more text per page, increased use of punctuation, greater variation in sentence patterns, and increasingly challenging vocabulary.

Level 5 encourages children to move from "learning to read" to "reading to learn" by providing even more text, varied writing styles, and less familiar topics.

Whichever book is right for your reader, Blastoff! Readers are the perfect books to build confidence and encourage a love of reading that will last a lifetime!

This edition first published in 2017 by Bellwether Media, Inc.

No part of this publication may be reproduced in whole or in part without written permission of the publisher. For information regarding permission, write to Bellwether Media, Inc., Attention: Permissions Department, 5357 Penn Avenue South, Minneapolis, MN 55419.

Library of Congress Cataloging-in-Publication Data

Names: Oachs, Emily Rose, author.
Title: Uruguay / by Emily Rose Oachs.
Description: Minneapolis, MN : Bellwether Media, Inc., 2017. | Series:
   Blastoff! Readers: Exploring Countries | Includes bibliographical
   references and index.
Identifiers: LCCN 2015051372 | ISBN 9781626174061 (hardcover : alk. paper)
Subjects: LCSH: Uruguay–Juvenile literature.
Classification: LCC F2708.5 .O23 2017 | DDC 989.5–dc23
LC record available at http://lccn.loc.gov/2015051372

Printed in the United States of America, North Mankato, MN.

Contents

Brazil

Uruguay River

Uruguay

Montevideo

Río de la Plata

Atlantic Ocean

Argentina

N

W   E

S

Uruguay is a small country in South America. Shaped like a teardrop, it covers 68,037 square miles (176,215 square kilometers) on the continent's southeastern coast. Uruguay's northern and eastern borders touch Brazil. The Uruguay River forms the country's western border. It separates Uruguay from Argentina.

The waters of the Atlantic Ocean wash onto Uruguay's eastern shore. To the south is the wide Río de la Plata. Montevideo is Uruguay's capital and largest city. More than half of the country's population lives there. It stands where the Río de la Plata and the Atlantic Ocean meet.

Pampas

Rolling, grassy **plains**, called the Pampas, stretch across much of Uruguay. Small streams and rivers carve through them. Large ranches, called *estancias*, cover vast areas of the Pampas. Livestock graze on their land.

Small regions of low hills rise in the north. Farther south, the Cuchilla Grande curves from Brazil toward the southern coast. This string of **highlands** boasts Mount Catedral, the country's highest point. Low, **fertile** land follows Uruguay's southern coast. Farmers plant many crops in these rich soils. Sand **dunes**, beaches, **marshes**, and **lagoons** line the Atlantic Ocean. The country sees mild, moist weather year-round.

Atlantic coast

7

Most Uruguayans live near the Río de la Plata in southern Uruguay. This waterway is a funnel-shaped **estuary** shared with Argentina. It begins where the Paraná and Uruguay Rivers join. At its widest, 136 miles (219 kilometers) separate its northern and southern shores. There, it joins the Atlantic Ocean.

Leatherback sea turtles, La Plata dolphins, hammerhead sharks, and many types of fish call the Río de la Plata home. However, water **pollution** from cities and farms threatens these animals. Uruguayans are working hard to clean up the waterway and protect its animals.

fun fact

Both Montevideo and Buenos Aires, Argentina's capital, stand along the Río de la Plata!

leatherback sea turtle

hammerhead shark

Río de la Plata

greater rhea

Pampas fox

capybaras

Many types of birds make Uruguay their home. Rheas dart across Uruguay's grasslands. These large, flightless birds search for seeds, insects, and lizards. Also on the grasslands, burrowing owls nest in small dugouts. Near the coast, herons, flamingos, and other water birds wade in lagoons. American oystercatchers feast on shellfish found during low **tide**.

tiger heron

The Pampas are home to armadillos and foxes. Pampas deer bound across the grasslands, too. In riverside forests, margays perch on tree branches. Capybaras and coatis also live in the forests. Caimans lurk in the flowing waters of the Uruguay River. Fur seals bark and honk from rocky coasts.

Did you know?

Near Brazil, some Uruguayans speak a combination of Spanish and Portuguese. They call this mixed language Portuñol.

About 3.3 million people live within Uruguay's borders. Few people **native** to the area live in the country. Most Uruguayans have **ancestors** from Spain and Italy. Fewer than one out of every ten people has both European and native ancestors. These Uruguayans are called *mestizos*. A small number of people in Uruguay have African ancestors.

Roman Catholicism is the largest religion in Uruguay. A small Jewish community lives in Montevideo. Much of the population does not practice any religion. Spanish is the country's official language. But many speakers have an Italian **accent**.

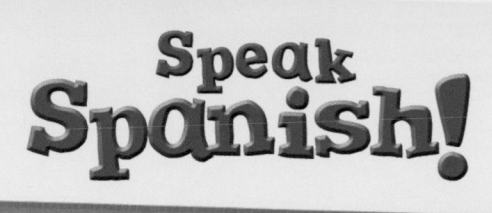

Speak Spanish!

English	Spanish	How to say it
hello	hola	OH-lah
good-bye	adiós	ah-dee-OHS
yes	sí	see
no	no	NOH
please	por favor	POHR fah-VOR
thank you	gracias	GRAH-see-uhs
friend (male)	amigo	ah-MEE-goh
friend (female)	amiga	ah-MEE-gah

Daily Life

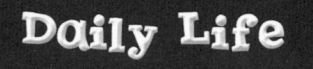

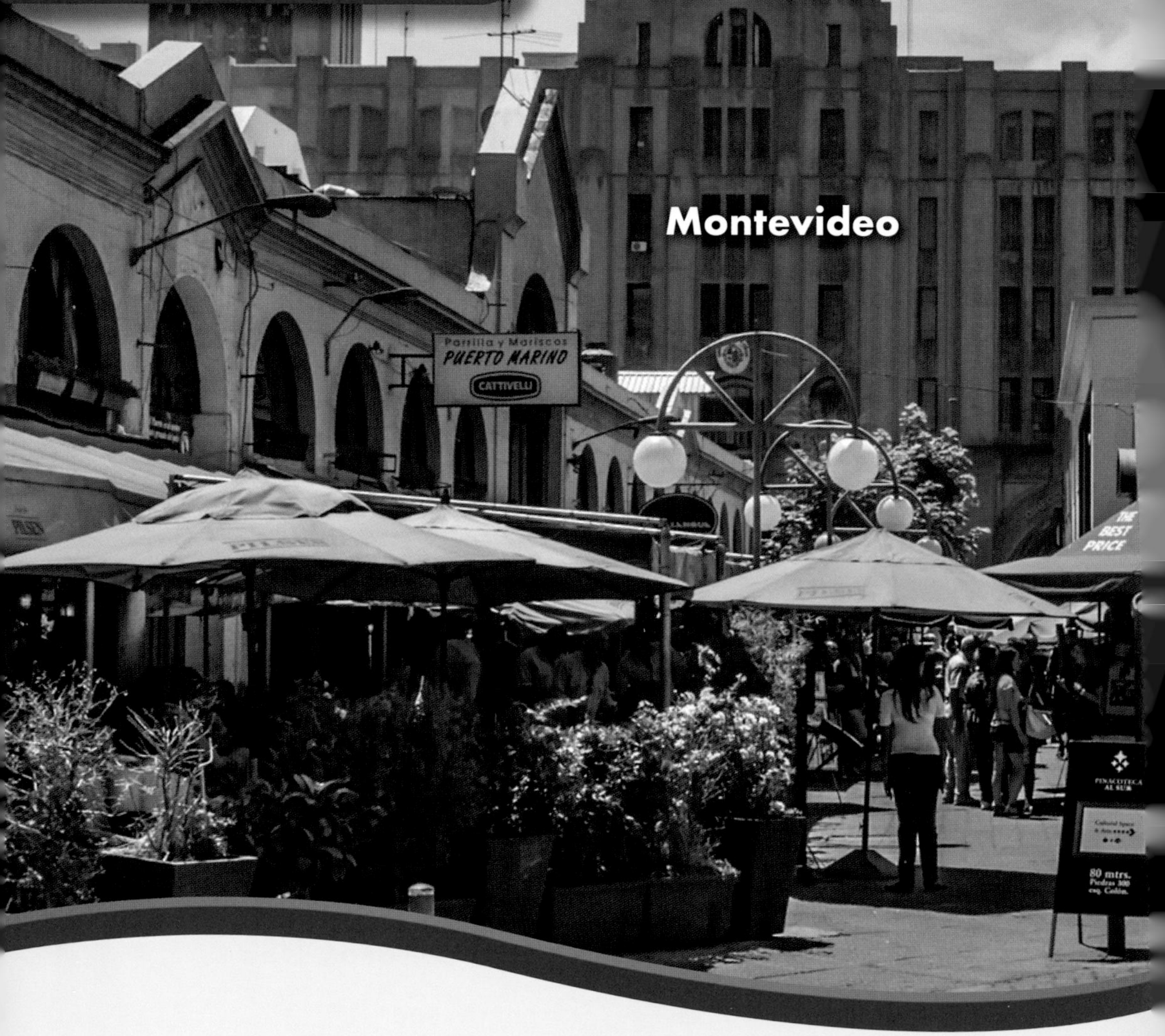

Montevideo

Most Uruguayans live in Montevideo and other cities along the southern coast. Many own their own homes, while others live in apartment buildings with other families. They take buses or drive cars to get from place to place. Both mothers and fathers often work outside the home. Grandparents may help with raising kids. Children are expected to help out by doing household chores.

The few Uruguayans in the countryside often live on ranches. They build their homes from **adobe** or brick and tin. Children may help out with caring for livestock. In the country, people use cars to get around. Highways connect the country's cities and towns. Some unpaved roads cut through the countryside.

Where People Live in Uruguay

countryside
4.7%

cities
95.3%

Did you know?

Small towns often do not have their own secondary schools. Students must then commute to nearby towns to continue their schooling.

Uruguay has one of the best education systems in South America. The government pays for public school all the way through university. Children must enter preschool at age 4. At age 6, they begin primary school. There, students learn how to read and write in Spanish. They also take classes in math and natural science.

After six years of primary school, students attend three years of lower secondary school. Then they continue with three years of higher secondary school. There, some students continue their general studies. Others choose to learn about a specific job. Graduates of secondary school find jobs or enroll in a university.

Where People Work in Uruguay

services 73%

manufacturing 14%

agriculture 13%

Most Uruguayans hold **service jobs**. They may work in shops, restaurants, hotels, or banks. Some are doctors, government workers, or teachers. Uruguayans also serve **tourists** at beachside **resorts**.

Much of the country's land is used for farming and ranching. Huge ranches raise cattle and sheep. The country **exports** a great deal of wool, beef, and livestock. Near the coast, farmers plant wheat and sugarcane. Other Uruguayan farmers grow corn, rice, and sunflowers. Factory workers make beef products, fabric, leather products, and chemicals. Uruguayan miners dig up small amounts of gold, gravel, iron, and sand.

soccer

Did you know?

In 1930, Uruguay hosted and won the first ever World Cup. They won it again in 1950!

Uruguayans are obsessed with soccer. Children learn to play when they are very young. They kick around a tin can or a rock if they have no soccer ball. Young and old alike cheer on the Uruguayan national team. They watch it on television or live from the stands.

In their free time, Uruguayans visit with friends in cafés. On weekends, they may gather for barbecues called *asados*. Children often play video games and watch movies with friends. In the countryside, people enjoy *payadas*, an old **tradition** from Uruguay's *gauchos*, or cowboys. During *payadas*, guitarists compete to make up new verses to the same song.

fun fact

Many people know the tango as a dance from Argentina. But musicians and dancers in Montevideo helped in the creation, too!

asado

Because Uruguay produces a lot of cattle, many Uruguayan dishes feature beef. Uruguayans love to eat *asado*, or grilled meat. To make it, cooks barbecue meat and organs on a special grill called a *parrilla*. *Chivitos* are also a popular food. These sandwiches are made with steak, eggs, cheese, and mayonnaise. Cooks prepare *puchero* stews using meat and vegetables. Small pies filled with meat or cheese called *empanadas* are a favorite snack.

Homemade pastas also make their way into Uruguayan meals. Spaghetti, lasagna, and gnocchi came to the country with Italian settlers. Uruguay's national drink is *maté*. This special tea is served in a **gourd**. Uruguayans drink it with a metal straw.

puchero

empanadas

In Montevideo, the Christian celebration of *Carnaval* in late winter lasts for more than a month! Uruguayans celebrate with musical street theater called *murga*. Parades of drummers and dancers take over the streets with *candombe* music. In the days before Easter, gauchos show off their skills in rodeos during Criolla Week. They compete in horseback riding and cattle roping.

Carnaval

! fun fact

Many Uruguayans celebrate Christmas with their loved ones. The government's official name for the holiday is the "Day of the Family." This is to include non-Christian families in the holiday.

Each August 25, Uruguayans celebrate the date they gained independence from Brazil. They wave flags, watch parades, and enjoy beautiful fireworks displays. November 2 is the Day of the Dead. On this day, Uruguayans visit graveyards and light candles to honor late relatives. Big parades feature Uruguayans dressed in bright clothes or skeleton costumes.

Uruguay's gauchos ride across the rolling Pampas. For more than 200 years, gauchos have worked there. First, they hunted wild cattle. Eventually, they began to herd sheep and cattle for large ranches. They wore loose pants, wide-brimmed hats, and ponchos. Many of today's gauchos still wear these traditional outfits.

Gauchos hold an important place in Uruguay's history and culture today. Gaucho rodeos draw large crowds. Younger generations learn gaucho history through ballads, folktales, and art. Uruguayans also respect gauchos for being well-mannered and polite. Many see gauchos as a **symbol** for Uruguay. They stand for their country's free spirit, courage, loyalty, and independence.

! fun fact

Early gauchos often used bolas to hunt rheas on the Pampas. A *bola* is made up of three stone balls attached to a leather rope. Gauchos would throw a bola so it wrapped around a rhea's legs.

gaucho rodeo

Did you know?
In the countryside, Uruguayan artists carve scenes into *maté* gourds. Gauchos and their lives are common subjects in these images.

Fast Facts About Uruguay

Uruguay's Flag

Uruguay's flag features nine horizontal stripes of white and blue. In the top left corner, a yellow sun with a face sits in a white square. The stripes symbolize the country's original nine departments, or states. The sun stands for the country's independence.

Official Name: Oriental Republic of Uruguay

Area: 68,037 square miles (176,215 square kilometers); Uruguay is the 91st largest country in the world.

Capital City:	Montevideo
Important Cities:	Salto, Paysandú, Ciudad de la Costa
Population:	3,341,893 (July 2015)
Official Language:	Spanish
National Holiday:	Independence Day (August 25)
Religions:	Roman Catholic (47.1%), non-Catholic Christians (11.1%), Jewish (0.3%), none (17.2%), other (24.3%)
Major Industries:	farming, manufacturing, services, tourism
Natural Resources:	farmland, gold, iron, gravel, fish
Manufactured Products:	food products, wool, fabric
Farm Products:	milk, beef, wool, rice, corn, wheat
Unit of Money:	Uruguayan peso; the peso is divided into 100 centésimos.

Glossary

accent—a way of speaking particular to a group of people, especially to the residents of a region

adobe—bricks made of clay and straw that are dried in the sun

ancestors—relatives who lived long ago

dunes—hills of sand

estuary—a waterway where the tide meets a river current

exports—sells to a different country

fertile—able to support growth

gourd—a large fruit with hard skin

highlands—areas of land that are higher than the surrounding land

lagoons—shallow bodies of seawater separated from the ocean

marshes—areas of wet land covered in grasses

native—originally from a specific place

plains—large areas of flat land

pollution—substances that make an area dirty or unusable

resorts—vacation spots that offer recreation, entertainment, and relaxation

service jobs—jobs that perform tasks for people or businesses

symbol—something that stands for something else

tide—the rising and falling of ocean water caused by the moon's position; the tide rises and falls twice each day.

tourists—people who travel to visit another place

tradition—a custom, idea, or belief handed down from one generation to the next

To Learn More

AT THE LIBRARY

Kortmeier, Todd. *Inside the World Cup.* Mankato, Minn.: Child's World, 2016.

Shields, Charles J. *Uruguay.* Bromall, Pa.: Mason Crest Publishers, 2009.

Sojo, Cecilia I. *The Everything Kids' Learning Spanish Book.* Avon, Mass.: Adams Media, 2010.

ON THE WEB

Learning more about Uruguay is as easy as 1, 2, 3.

1. Go to www.factsurfer.com.

2. Enter "Uruguay" into the search box.

3. Click the "Surf" button and you will see a list of related web sites.

With factsurfer.com, finding more information is just a click away.

Index